In the Sun King's
Paris
with Molière

COME SEE MY CITY

In the Sun King's
Paris
with Molière

Text by Renzo Rossi
Illustrations by Alessandro Baldanzi

Marshall Cavendish
Benchmark

New York

This edition first published in 2009 in North America by Marshall Cavendish Benchmark.

Marshall Cavendish Benchmark
99 White Plains Road
Tarrytown, NY 10591
www.marshallcavendish.us

Library of Congress Cataloging-in-Publication Data

Rossi, Renzo, 1940–
In the Sun King's Paris with Molière / by Renzo Rossi.
    p. cm. — (Come see my city)
  ISBN 978-0-7614-4332-2
  1. Louis XIV, King of France, 1638–1715—Juvenile literature. 2. Molière, 1622–1673—Juvenile literature. 3. Paris (France)—History—1589–1789—Juvenile literature. 4. Paris (France)—Social life and customs—17th century—Juvenile literature. 5. France—History—Louis XIV, 1643–1715—Juvenile literature. I. Title.
    DC729.R67 2009
    944–dc22

                                2008032321

Text: Renzo Rossi
Translation: Erika Pauli
Illustrations: Alessandro Baldanzi

Photographs: pp. 7, 21, 43 Scala Archives, Florence

Printed in Malaysia
1 3 5 6 4 2

contents

Our Guide:

Molière

On January 15, 1622, Jean-Baptiste Poquelin, first-born son of the upholsterer for the royal house-hold, was baptized in the church of Saint Eustache near the ancient markets (Les Halles). The Poquelins had been upholsterers for three generations. They were not humble artisans, but solid middle-class citizens with a successful business serving dukes and princes. Master Poquelin saw to the maintenance of the wall coverings in all the royal residences. He also helped the chamber valets make the bed of the king, **Louis XIII**.

The Poquelins were wealthy enough to send young Jean-Baptiste to Clermont, an exclusive college run by the **Jesuits**, and to Orléans, where he received a law degree. Though he was a lawyer, Poquelin rarely argued cases in court; he preferred to befriend companies of itinerant actors, especially that of the Béjart. Poquelin had a passion for the stage, but he was also drawn by the artful charms of the leading lady, Madeleine Béjart, who became a lifelong companion. At twenty-one, Poquelin decided to devote himself to the stage and founded the Illustre Théâtre company with Béjart. So as not to embarrass his family, he took Molière as his stage name.

The Illustre Théâtre was a small, modest company with little financial backing. After a promising start in Rouen, the company began performing in Paris, but was soon in debt. To keep creditors at bay, Molière borrowed money from his forgiving father, but a few times he also was thrown into the Paris prisons. After two years the Illustre Théâtre company broke up and Molière, with Béjart and a few other performers, started traveling to the provinces to perform. During his thirteen years as a traveling actor, Molière learned to direct and wrote his first two comedies: *L'Étourdi ou les contretemps* (*The Blunderer*) in 1655 and *Le Dépit amoureux* (*The Amorous Quarrel*) in 1656. Though he was the chief actor of the itinerant group, Molière seems to have been only mediocre.

Ambition kept pace with experience and, in 1658, the company decided to attempt the great Paris adventure again. Under the official protection of the duc d'Orléans, the king's brother, the company of vagabond actors was given the Petit-Bourbon, the theater inside the Louvre. At that time there were two other permanent theaters in Paris: the one in the Hôtel de Bourgogne where the King's Company performed, and the Marais Theater, where the company founded by Montdory, famous for his passionate acting, performed. Audiences at the Petit-Bourbon went wild for Molière's comedies, which highlighted and ridiculed the weaknesses, vices, hypocrisy, defects, and errors of society.

In 1662, at the age of forty, Molière married Armande Béjart, seventeen-year-old sister (although some said the daughter) of Madeleine. The age difference soon caused problems: she was a flirt and he was a jealous husband. Molière transferred the situation to his comedy *L'École des femmes* (*The School for Wives*). In 1664, when the palace of Versailles was inaugurated, Molière staged *Tartuffe*, a satire on hypocrisy that targeted religion, its practices, and its followers. The subject scandalized the clergy and the conformists, who raised obstacles to its performance for five years. Other masterpieces followed: *Dom Juan, ou le festin de Pierre* (*Don Juan, or the Feast with the Statue*) (1665), *The Misanthrope* (*The Miser*) (1668), *Le Malade imaginaire* (*The Imaginary Invalid*) (1673).

Above: A group of actors with the Comédie Française, the national theater, in a painting by Jean-Antoine Watteau.

At the fourth presentation of his last comedy, on February 17, 1673, Molière collapsed on stage; he barely managed to complete his part and died a few hours later. The priest of Saint Eustache, where Molière had been baptized, refused to inter him in consecrated earth. The bishop of Paris intervened and allowed Molière's body to be buried on the outskirts of a cemetery, at night and without ceremony.

Map of the City

There's little left of seventeenth-century Paris. Most of the Paris that Molière and the Sun King knew was lost when the city was restructured in the nineteenth century. Great monuments, such as Notre Dame and the Louvre, survived, but have been modified in answer to new needs. The fortifications, narrow winding medieval streets, and medieval bridges are things of the past.

Today the symbols of Paris are more recent monuments, like the Eiffel Tower, the Arc de Triomphe on the Champs-Elysées, and the Pantheon, where the great men of France are buried.

Over the centuries the city expanded, merging with surrounding suburbs. Saint-Cloud, Saint-Denis, and Vincennes were once surrounded by thick forests, but are now part of the urban layout.

Boulevard Haussmann

Arc de Triomphe

Avenue des Champs-Elysées

Grand Palais

Place de La Concorde

Seine

Jardin de Tuileries

Tour Eiffel

Hôtel des Invalides

Musée d'Orsay

Parc du Champ-de-Mars

10

MONTPARNASSE

Cimettère de Montparnass

Place de la Porte de Versailles

TO VERSAILLES

11

12

13

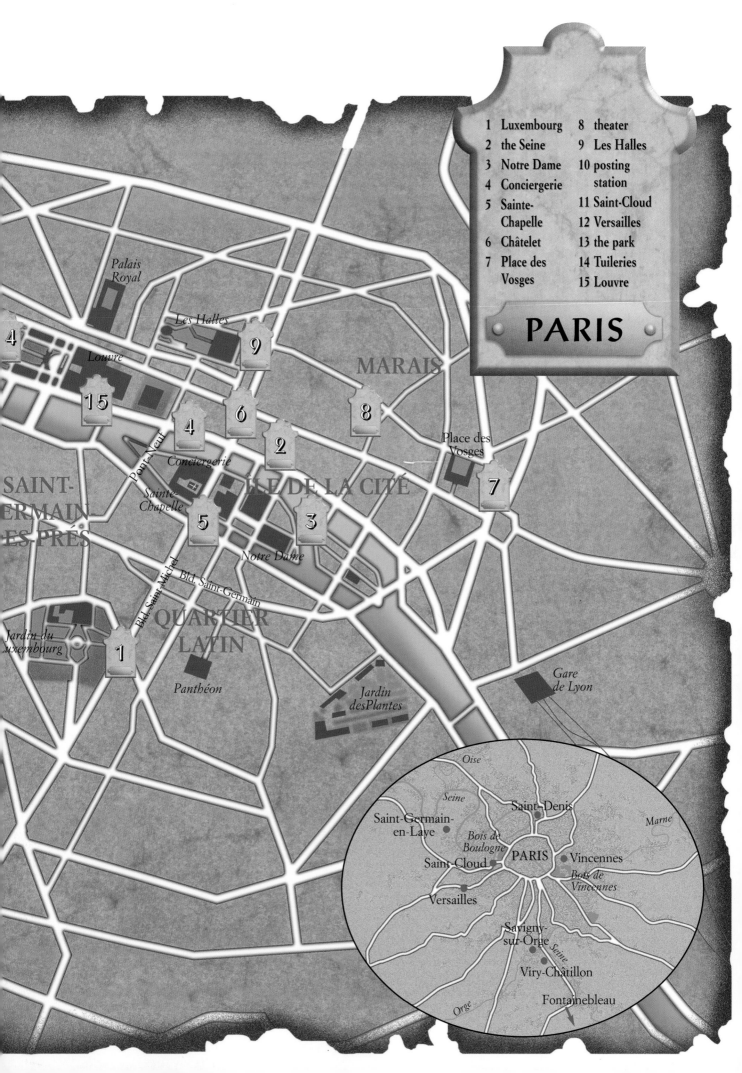

Palais
Royal

Les Halles

Louvre

SAINT-
GERMAIN-
DES-PRÉS

Pont-Neuf

Conciergerie

Sainte-
Chapelle

Bld. Saint-Michel

Bld. Saint-Germain

QUARTIER
LATIN

Jardin du
Luxembourg

Panthéon

MARAIS

Place des
Vosges

ÎLE DE LA CITÉ

Notre Dame

Jardin
des Plantes

Gare
de Lyon

1 Luxembourg
2 the Seine
3 Notre Dame
4 Conciergerie
5 Sainte-
  Chapelle
6 Châtelet
7 Place des
  Vosges

8 theater
9 Les Halles
10 posting
   station
11 Saint-Cloud
12 Versailles
13 the park
14 Tuileries
15 Louvre

PARIS

Oise

Seine

Saint-Denis

Saint-Germain-
en-Laye

Bois de
Boulogne

Marne

Saint-Cloud

PARIS

Vincennes

Bois de
Vincennes

Versailles

Savigny-
sur-Orge

Seine

Viry-Châtillon

Orge

Fontainebleau

Paris!

My name is Frank, I'm thirteen years old, and I'm in Paris all by myself. Well, almost by myself. My parents aren't with me, but my Uncle Mike and Aunt Louise have lived here for more than ten years, and then there's my cousin Brigitte, who was born in Paris. I come for visits quite often and they come see us every now and then, too. No doubt about it, though, I get the better deal.

Paris is really cool! Have you ever seen anything like Île de la Cité, the island in the Seine? It's the historical center of the city and has more great monuments, like the cathedral of Notre Dame, than anywhere else. Well, actually there are two islands, Île de la Cité, and the smaller Île Saint-Louis. A total of twelve bridges join them to the two banks of the Seine. Uncle Mike once said, "The Seine divides Paris into two symbolic worlds. The right bank represents the world of business, elegance, and trade. The **left bank** is full of culture: the University of Paris–Sorbonne, bookshops, and theaters."

To help me understand Paris better, my uncle also explained that in the middle of the nineteenth century the city was drastically transformed. Emperor **Napoleon III** wanted to have the most beautiful capital in the world and commissioned prefect **Baron Haussmann** to give Paris a face-lift. The medieval walls and narrow, winding streets of the old city were replaced with broad avenues and the large, spacious squares of which Parisians are so proud. Many old buildings were restored or rebuilt according to their original architecture.

"The city we have today is partly real and partly imagined," said my uncle, "but if you look hard enough there are several versions of Paris, each one just as fascinating as the next: Gothic and medieval Paris of kings such as **Henry IV** and Louis XIV; that of the **French Revolution** of 1789; the Paris of the late-nineteenth century, which is recognized by the iron architecture of the Eiffel Tower and some bridges and railroad stations; the artists' Paris in Montmartre; and the Paris of the future in the new district of the Défense."

I was happy with my cousin Brigitte's Paris, though. I knew that, given the chance, the two of us would discover all kinds of interesting things.

Pont au Change

Conciergerie

Palais de Justice

Place Dauphine

Pont-Neuf

Square du Vert Galant

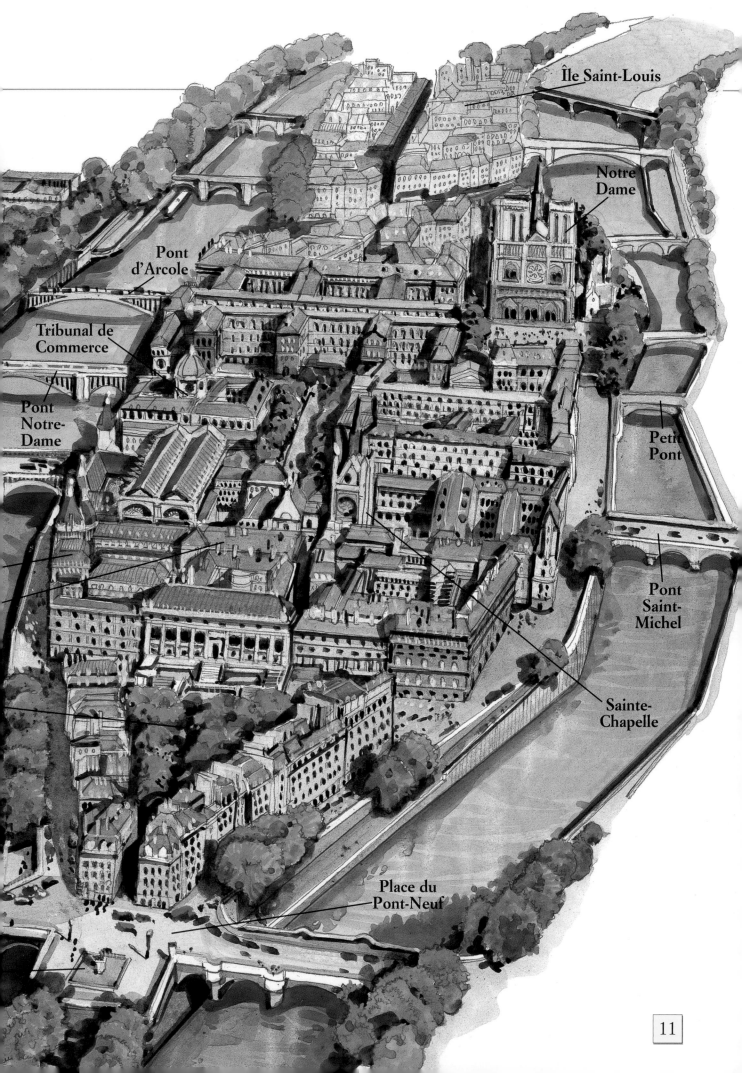

Île Saint-Louis

Notre Dame

Pont d'Arcole

Tribunal de Commerce

Pont Notre-Dame

Petit Pont

Pont Saint-Michel

Sainte-Chapelle

Place du Pont-Neuf

11

A Gentleman from the Past

Brigitte and I spent most of our time in the Luxembourg Gardens, which was practically next door to her home. Brigitte knew a lot about the place and told me that **Marie de' Medici**, a noblewoman from Florence, Italy, once lived in the palace overlooking the park. The senate meets there now. We always found plenty to do in our mornings at the park, ambling along between the flowerbeds of dahlias and scarlet sage, reading on the lawn in the midst of orange trees and oleanders, or watching the old men play chess under the elm trees. Sometimes we helped other kids sail their boats in the little lake where a stone **Triton** spouts water. Just about every day we would end up in front of the small, brightly decorated puppet theater to watch Punchinello and Harlequin beat each other up.

Every time we went to the gardens, we noticed a man a little ways off in clothes that were even odder than those of the puppets. He wore a wide-brimmed felt hat with a feather, a purple cape, knee-length breeches, white stockings, and shoes with heels. One day he came over and started to talk to us. "I adore the theater, all kinds of theater, including this one. Let me introduce myself: Monsieur Molière, at your service. You may even have seen some of my plays."

I shrugged my shoulders, embarrassed, but Brigitte answered excitedly: "Are you really Molière? I know the plot of *The Miser* and my mother says it's just great."

"Merci. In that case I must show you a truly great theater. It's not all that close, but on our way I can show you the greatest stage on earth: my Paris."

My uncle's words came to mind and I answered enthusiastically, "We can't miss this for anything!"

"Then let the curtain rise!" exclaimed Molière.

Along the Seine

"This, my dear children, is one of the most fabulous views of the Seine. Can you imagine a more fascinating backdrop for a play than Pont Notre-Dame? Magnificent and indomitable," said Molière when we arrived at the river.

"It really is a wonderful bridge, Monsieur Molière," said Brigitte, "but I'm afraid it doesn't exist any more. Why do you talk about the bridge as if it were a stage set?"

"All of life's a stage," answered our guide unhesitatingly, "and you, mademoiselle, are an impatient spectator. Be good enough to let me continue. I said 'indomitable' for a reason, for Pont Notre-Dame has collapsed and been rebuilt three times in the course of just a hundred years. To pay for the last reconstruction, which was in 1500, the city had to impose a special tax on fish, cattle, and salt. The bridge has six 56-foot (17-m) stone arches that support sixty-five symmetrical brick and stone houses!"

"Awesome! But those houses don't look very safe to me," I said, a bit doubtful.

"Safe? Mon Dieu, they couldn't be safer!" laughed Molière. "And in great demand. Each house has a storeroom set right into the arch, a shop that overlooks the street, and three living floors. The inhabitants are mostly booksellers, hatmakers, and tailors."

"And those big wheels at water level?" asked Brigitte.

"Waterwheels, my dear. The waterwheels power the mills where we grind our wheat into flour. Almost every bridge has some."

Molière's eyes sparkled as he told us of the last time the king and his court had entered Paris, passing over the bridge on their way to Notre Dame to offer a prayer of thanksgiving before continuing on to the Louvre.

"You should have seen the houses," he added, "tapestries were hanging out all the windows and garlands were draped along the whole route. The streets were even covered with carpets!"

The Cathedral of Notre Dame

When we got to the cathedral of Notre Dame, Brigitte couldn't believe her eyes. She often came here, and the square was much smaller than the one she was used to.

"I suppose things do change. I can, however, give you a bit of history," said Molière. "Ages ago there was a Gallo-Roman temple to Jupiter here. Then, when Christianity arrived, two churches were built on the site—one was a church to the Virgin Mary. It was fairly small, but in 1150 the splendor of Louis VII's reign demanded something more imposing. The new, gigantic structure changed the whole layout of the Cité. Over the next hundred years, four different architects had a hand in the building, each one adding his own ideas. By 1230 the Notre Dame de Paris, Our Lady of Paris, that you see now was complete."

"One thing that hasn't changed is the confusion," said Brigitte, more interested in the people than the church.

"Have you ever seen anything like that rose window?" Molière went on, paying no attention to her. "It's 31 feet (9.5 m) in diameter and acts as a sort of halo for the statue of the Virgin inside. And the façade! A real masterpiece of stage design, with the horizontal galleries acting as a platform for two towers. Can you imagine what it would have been like if they had been finished?"

"You mean they were supposed to be even taller?" I asked.

"Yes, two spires reaching heavenward were originally planned," answered Molière, pointing dramatically up to the sky. "The façade of a church is a great book, a theater in stone. It's a mirror of nature, instruction, morals, and history. The story of the lives of Mary and Jesus Christ, the Last Judgment, the virtues and vices, the labors of man, the seven arts—"

I think he would have kept on forever if Brigitte hadn't run over to watch the fire-eaters.

"Don't go off too far, ma chère," cautioned Molière. "This is the favorite stage of acrobats, storytellers, jugglers, and fire-eaters, as well as pickpockets."

"You know, Monsieur Molière," Brigitte interrupted as she bent down to pet a small dog that had wandered over, "maybe things really haven't changed that much."

The Caretaker's Palace

The whole western part of the Île de la Cité was covered buildings in all different architectural styles. We stopped in front of two imposing round towers with steepled roofs and Molière explained that the kings of France, especially those in the thirteenth and fourteenth centuries, had constantly added to and transformed these buildings.

"In the late Roman period," said Molière, "the governor had his headquarters here. It was transformed into a fortified royal residence in the eighth century. And since this was where the king was, this was where the law courts and prisons had to be. When the kings moved to other residences, the entire complex became the Palace of Justice. What we're looking at is only half of the right wing, known as the *conciergerie*."

"That means 'caretaker's lodge,'" Brigitte translated for me. "Monsieur Molière, isn't it much too big a building to be simply a caretaker's lodge. Why do they call it that?"

"You must remember, ma petite mademoiselle, that the concierge who lived here was not a porter or caretaker in the normal sense. He was the superintendent of the king, a sort of governor of the city, who enjoyed broad powers and privileges. The state treasury and the administration of justice also fell under his jurisdiction. Take these towers for instance. They date back to the fourteenth century. The first is the Tour d'Argent, or Silver Tower, which still houses the royal treasury; it is also used as a prison, like its twin tower, Tour de César, or Caesar's Tower. They were built on the foundations of a Roman bastion."

"Is the square tower a prison, too?" I asked.

"No, that's the Clock Tower, built by Philip the Fair, king of France around 1300. The great clock on the other side was the first of its kind in Paris. But it keeps stopping. They're always repairing it, but it doesn't seem to make any difference."

"Can we go in, Monsieur Molière?" asked Brigitte.

"We must! There's an absolutely marvelous masterpiece of architecture no one should miss in the courtyard. Let's go and see Sainte-Chapelle."

The Holy Chapel

As we crossed the courtyards and galleries of the various buildings in the Palace of Justice, Molière told us the story of the Sainte-Chapelle. It was built between 1241 and 1248 for **Louis IX**, who then died in the Crusades and was proclaimed a saint. "It contains the relics of the crucifixion of Christ," said our guide reverently, "including the crown of thorns."

"But the fact that the Saint-Chapelle is inside the palace walls gives it another meaning as well," explained Molière. "It is a political and religious statement. Louis IX wanted to emphasize his double function as both temporal and spiritual head of a people and that his task was to lead them to eternal salvation."

On one side of a large courtyard stood a building with pointed arches and a tall spire. It was an unbelievable structure, not only because it was so high and airy, but also because of the stained-glass windows. It looked like a brilliant bubble of colored glass, an enormous and wonderful **reliquary**.

"This is a masterpiece of thirteenth-century Gothic architecture," said Molière. "There is the lower chapel for the public, and an upper chapel reserved for the king."

We entered a hall with what looked like a forest of columns painted blue, red, and gold.

THE STAINED-GLASS WINDOWS

This stained-glass window in Sainte-Chapelle (*left*) depicts the coronation of a king and is one of many in Sainte-Chapelle. Gothic architecture used a great deal of stained glass. The light that filtered through the brilliantly colored panes gave the church a serene, meditative, and beautiful atmosphere. At the same time, the windows illustrated sacred stories, like earlier mosaics and frescoes, that the faithful could "read" during services.

"There are forty columns," said Molière, "and they support the ribbed **vaulting** that supports the upper chapel. Lords and prelates are buried under the floor. Actually, it was in this room that the king and members of the court confessed their sins to the priest before going to the upper chapel where the relics are kept."

"Have you ever seen it?" asked Brigitte.

"I was allowed to enter once, together with other courtiers. There are fifteen dazzling stained-glass windows that narrate the stories of the Old Testament. There are also gilded wooden angels and statues of the twelve apostles. And, of course, the rose window. But what moved me most was the canopy at the back of the **apse** where relics of the Passion, Christ's crucifixion, are on view in a wooden shrine."

The Castle that Once Was

When we left Île de la Cité, we found ourselves in front of a massive fortified building.

"There's no castle like this here any more. This is supposed to be Châtelet Square!" exclaimed Brigitte in astonishment.

"This is the Grand Châtelet," explained Molière, "the fortress was built around 1100 to defend the entrance to the Cité on the right bank of the Seine. There is another fort, the Petit Châtelet, on the left bank. The Grand Châtelet is the seat of the prefect of Paris, the highest ranking judge, and his court of justice. His prison is famous for the tortures inflicted here. There's one funnel-shaped room where prisoners have to stand all the time. It's the gloomiest building in Paris and I'm not the least sorry if, as you say, it was torn down."

"People don't seem to mind that it's gloomy," I said looking around. "The street is very lively."

"That's because we're at a crossroads," explained Molière. "This is where the crier calls out ordinances, prices of the merchandise, names of those who died that day, and other news. It's like a town square. There are craftsmen making and selling their wares and workers offering their services. Anything you need for daily life can be found here."

"What's that horrible smell?" said Brigitte, wrinkling her nose.

"That's the slaughter house," said Molière in a disgusted tone. "Every butcher brings his animals here and slaughters them himself. You'll also find tripe shops, tanneries, and dyers. The liquid refuse from all these processes go into that drainage canal at the center of the street and flow into the Seine. To say the least, it's not the best place for one's health. The king, who wants his city to be clean, sometimes threatens to walk through the streets to check up on the state of affairs. Then everybody cleans and tidies up, but before long it's back to what it was."

"What do people do about their ... refuse?" I asked, embarrassed.

Molière laughed and shrugged his shoulders. "Here at the Châtelet, the landlords ignore regulations and don't provide latrines and sewage pits, even when twenty or more families live in their buildings. The tenants simply throw the contents of their chamber pots out the windows, crying, 'Watch out below!'"

A Pedestrian Mall

The name of the Marais quarter tells us what used to be here—*marais* means "swamps" in French. The land was drained for farming in the twelfth century. In Molière's time, as he explained, it was the fashionable place for the aristocracy to build elegant homes called *hôtels*. After passing through a series of winding but well-maintained streets we came to a square that Molière called Place Royale. Brigitte knew it as Place des Vosges.

"The name was changed," Brigitte explained to Molière, "by an emperor named **Napoleon Bonaparte**. But it doesn't matter much what it's called. Tell us how it came to be."

"There used to be a royal residence known as the Hôtel de Tournelles here. In 1559, unfortunately for the hôtel, **Henry II** died inside its walls after being wounded in a joust. His widow, the Italian **Catherine de' Medici**, had the palace razed to the ground. Eventually the location was used for a horse market."

"A funny way to get even," I said, astounded.

"Queen Catherine loved her husband; she wore black for thirty years after his death," explained Molière.

"This still doesn't tell us how this square came to be," said my cousin.

"At the beginning of this century King Henry IV, the grandfather of my King Louis XIV, set up a silk factory on the north side of this square space, and on the other three sides had the lodgings for the workers built," explained Molière. "The factory soon went out of business and the square became a place where people gather to socialize, a sort of pedestrian mall, and was called Place Royale."

The square was perfectly symmetrical. The buildings all had steep, gabled roofs covered in slate. I counted them: thirty-six total, nine on each side. Molière noticed and explained: "Henry IV set up precise rules for the buildings: the height of the roofs and the alignment of the façades were meant to be architecturally unifying. He kept that raised pavilion, known as the King's Pavilion, which is the only unsymmetrical feature, for himself. As you see, Place Royale is popular. I wouldn't advise you to come here at dawn though. This is a popular place for duels, even though the king has prohibited them."

Passion for the Theater

After leaving Place Royale, Molière dragged us to a place that, he explained, had once been a covered tennis court and was now the Marais Theater.

"Ah! The stage!" exclaimed Molière. "Can you smell it? It's intoxicating and unmistakable."

The smell of the place might have been intoxicating for a man of the theater like Molière, and it was certainly unmistakable. It smelled of dust, sweat, unwashed clothing, wine, and garlic. It almost made me choke.

"It's mostly the common people who come here to the Marais Theater," explained Molière. "They know what they want: if it's a tragedy, they expect to weep and if it's a comedy or farce, they expect to laugh. One of each is performed every evening."

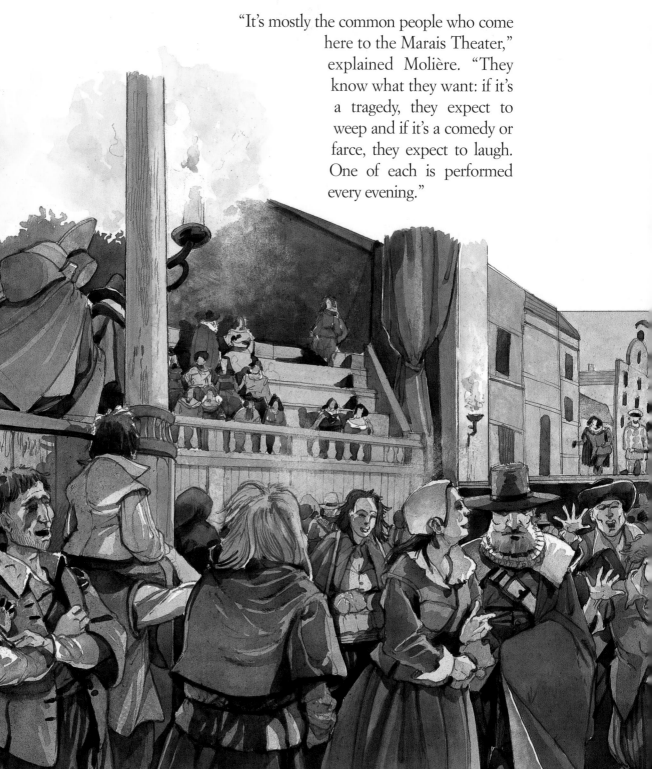

"Does the audience stand the whole time?" asked Brigitte.

"Only in the pit," explained Molière. "That way it's easier to move from one group to another and talk about the play, quarrel when they don't agree, or go out and buy food and drink. The few boxes and the balconies are for the wealthy upper classes, for the ladies, and for the aristocrats who don't want to associate with the lower classes. When particularly important spectators come, they are seated in cane chairs right on the side of the stage."

"I've never seen such confusion," I shouted to make myself heard above the racket. "How does the audience manage to follow what's going on?"

"Most of those who are here have already seen the play at least a dozen times, and the actors are chosen because of their powerful voices. But this evening the audience does seem particularly enthralled. Every so often there is a brawl and even a duel. Once a woman had her baby right here in the pit, but the audience barely noticed, and she certainly didn't want to go away before the end of the play."

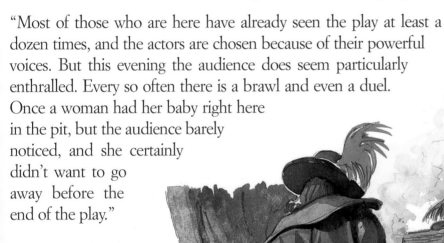

The Belly of Paris

We took a short walk to the liveliest, most colorful place that I had ever seen or imagined. All sorts of activities were going on.

"Here we are at Les Halles," he said gaily, "the stage where the daily life of the common people is played out. I could use this as the setting for some great plays."

"It looks to me like the whole quarter is a food market," I said looking around.

"It is the belly of Paris," explained our guide. "Everything eaten in the city first passes through here and is then distributed to retailers. The two large pavilions behind the fountain in the center are the fish and salt markets. The street behind them is called Cheese Street. I don't have to tell you why. Then there is the grain market, the meat market, the legume market—"

"What do they sell in that tower?" asked Brigitte.

"They don't sell anything there," said Molière laughing. "Shame and humiliation is the price you pay when you're put in the **stocks** there and exposed to public scorn."

"But who gets put up there and why?" Brigitte wanted to know.

"Dishonest merchants—those who cheat their customers, evade taxes, or adulterate their wares. If you mix marble dust into the salt you sell, sooner or later you'll end up in the stocks. Every so often petty swindlers, pickpockets, or money lenders are hoisted up there to serve as an example. Les Halles has to have a reputation for being safe or people won't come. A dishonest merchant dishonors the market, and discredits commerce. The king's men are keeping their eyes on everyone and have informants as well."

A Tavern Snack

All the walking had made Brigitte and I tired, hungry, and thirsty. We timidly asked if we couldn't take a short rest.

"I thought you might be ready for one," said Molière smiling. "Let's go over there. *A la jolie Laitière* is both a tavern and a post station. So we'll fill our stomachs first and then I'll take you by coach to Versailles."

"You merit applause, my good sir," I recited theatrically. "You have all the approval and gratitude of your public."

"Come on, my clever clown," Molière laughed, "we have no time to waste. Versailles is quite a ways from here."

10

The tavern was a large, well-lit vaulted room. There were wooden tables and stools scattered about, but all of them were taken. "You can tell a good tavern by how animated the customers are," said Molière. "Seems to me this tavern passes the test. We'll get something to drink—my throat is dry from all this talking—then the house specialty: sausages from Périgord, cheese from Normandy, meatloaf, fish patties, hard-boiled eggs, ham, and salted herring. Maybe not the cookies and cream pie—we don't want to be too full."

We looked at each other and all three of us broke out laughing.

Through the Woods by Coach

We excitedly climbed into the coach that Molière had hired for the trip to Versailles. Molière was a real gentleman, no question. When we had comfortably settled down and were entering the dense woods of Saint-Cloud he began to tell us the story of Versailles, which he had christened the Enchanted Isle.

"You should know," he began, "that Louis XIII, the father of my king, was the first to take a liking to the land around Versailles, which he bought in 1627 for 20,000 **écus**. He built a modest castle to use as a hunting lodge. But the location was so fantastic, overlooking the **Île-de-France** region, that Louis XIV transformed the castle into an elaborate palace. It was Louis's personal masterpiece, for nothing was done that he had not designed, studied, discussed, and approved."

"King Louis must have been enthusiastic," I said.

"He was enthusiastic and he had the means, my son," continued Molière. "Work began in 1662. At the beginning, 30,000 men and 6,000 horses were working daily for the king. Many died in accidents at work, but even more died from disease. The area was hot and there was a lot of stagnant water. Every night the dead were secretly carried away so as not to alarm the other workers. Construction costs rose to dizzying heights each year: 5 million Tours pounds (almost the equivalent of 4 tons of gold) in 1669, 20 million in 1671, and **Jean-Baptiste Colbert**, the king's superintendent, was constantly worried by what he judged to be a colossal waste. But Louis wanted no criticism, money was not his problem. 'I am the king,' he said."

"Louis exhibited all his arrogance in Versailles. He found a swamp and turned it into the most splendid garden in Europe. When he didn't like the view, he transformed nature to create this panorama, commissioning three brilliant artists: architect Louis Le Vau, painter Charles Le Brun, and garden poet André Le Nôtre. You'll see the result shortly."

The Palace of the Sun King

"We'll enter the palace through one of the side pavilions," said Molière when we arrived at Versailles. "Actually, you're supposed to go through the Place d'Armes, which leads you to the majestic main façades. Even though the king comes here more frequently, there is still construction going on in many places."

"I thought it was a palace," I said amazed. "Looks more like an elegant city to me."

"That was the king's intention: take the **anagram** of Versailles: *ville seras*."

"It means 'you will be a city,'" Brigitte translated for me. "I bet you can easily get lost in here."

"Not with me," said Molière, "I know my way around. Act natural, smile at everyone, and if in doubt, bow or curtsy. Everyone at Versailles, including the pages, thinks highly of themselves."

"Monsieur Molière," said Brigitte, "they're all looking at us."

"Let them look and gossip," smiled our guide. "That's the most popular pastime here in court. But you are here as tourists and I therefore have to explain a few things to you. This part of the palace was all rebuilt by the architect Louis Le Vau, who is a good friend of mine. He designed a majestic stone façade and disguised the flat roof with decorated screens."

"What a place to live," I observed.
"Everyone seems to be in their best attire."

"My lad," said Molière, "this is a jungle. Life in Versailles is
a hymn to joy, but is a hotbed of intrigue because everything revolves
around the king, like the planets around the sun. Louis is called the Sun King,
after all. Every courtier wants to be noticed—it's his or her best chance at moving
up in society. But standing out, or even staying afloat, in a crowd of 10,000 courtiers
isn't easy."

The Park of Marvels

We were standing on the central terrace looking out over an immense park, which seemed to be divided into three zones. There were open gardens at the foot of the castle, then the lush, green woods, and, on the horizon, the natural forest. What struck us was the perfect geometry of the pathways. There were hedges, marble and bronze statues, and rows of pots with flourishing orange and lemon trees. Here and there the sun sparkled off the water of a fountain, pool, or canal.

"What you're marveling at is André Le Nôtre's masterpiece," said Molière, who was behind us. "I knew what I was talking about before when I called him the 'poet of gardens.'"

"I don't know if I'd call them gardens though. They're so perfect I'm almost afraid to touch anything. You know, like a museum," I said.

"Quite true, my friend. This is a carefully planned work of art," explained Molière. "Think of the conditions in which Le Nôtre had to work. He dried out these marshy zones and ended up with an empty stretch of land, a white page on which to lay out his project. He transplanted entire forests from Normandy and Flanders and had 50,000 bulbs sent from Constantinople. The troops of Louis XIV helped with it all. In fact, the pool was dug by a regiment of Swiss guards."

"The fountains and their water displays are really fantastic," said Brigitte.

"All the more so when you realize that this area has no natural source of water," Molière answered. "The water in the canals and fountains is brought by conduits from the Seine, several miles away. This is Apollo's Basin. The gilded bronze statue is of Apollo, the Sun god, in his chariot, surrounded by tritons and marine monsters, a clear reference to the Sun King."

"A place like this would be great for jogging," I observed. "But seriously, it's got to be used for something besides leisurely walks."

"Quite right," answered Molière. "You might call it an amusement park for the upper classes. There are parties, hunting excursions, ballets, and jousting. There was a seven-day inauguration celebration in 1664. I invented the celebration's title, 'The Pleasures of the Enchanted Isle.' The entire week this isle was the scene of allegorical processions in which Louis XIV appeared in a chariot wearing splendid silver armor, torch-light dances, music composed by court musician **Lully**, and ballets. The king himself danced in those—he was actually quite elegant. That was also when I was allowed to present my comedy *Tartuffe*, and the king had a great time."

The Palace of Tiles

There was an announcement that the king was about to leave Versailles for the city, so we hurried back to Paris. When we returned Molière took us to the Tuileries, which closed the great four-sided court of the Louvre.

"The Tuileries," he explained, "get their name from an old tile factory that once stood here. Queen Catherine had this palace built in the Italian style to remind her of her youth. The medieval huts here were all torn down, creating an immense space more suited to a park. Under Henry IV, two galleries were built to join the Louvre and the Tuileries: the Small Gallery, which begins at the Pavilion of Flora, and the Grand Gallery, which begins at the Pavilion of Marsan, the one you see there in front of us."

"The Louvre, the Tuileries, pavilions, galleries, and parks are all one great complex," I observed, "or maybe I should say an enormous construction yard, because there's work going on everywhere!"

"The kings and queens of France have always had 'brick fever,'" said Molière, laughing. "Louis XIII added to the Tuileries, so of course Louis XIV had to outdo his father."

"But the king loves Versailles," said Brigitte. "When he moves there permanently, what's going to happen to all this?"

"Pessimists say work will come to a halt. Perhaps the buildings will be used for academies or exhibitions. At worst, huts like the ones that were torn down may pop up again in the courtyards and gardens. Who knows?"

Just then a group of courtiers on horseback galloped into the courtyard, heading toward the opposite side of the square.

"The king is arriving!" exclaimed Molière. "I have to run to the Cour Carrée, the square court of the Louvre, to greet him. He would never forgive me if I didn't do my duty, and you never want to be on the king's bad side!"

Yesterday's Fortress, Today's Museum

"We've lost him, Brigitte," I said. "Molière left us without even saying good-bye."

"We certainly can't expect to be more important than the king," said Brigitte, shrugging her shoulders. "After all, Molière is a man of court and owes everything to the benevolence of Louis XIV."

"That's not what I mean—we didn't get a chance to thank him!"

"There he is, before His Majesty the Sun King. Let's just smile and wave. I'm sure he'll understand how grateful we are." As we waved the regal scene faded away and was replaced by tourists milling around taking pictures and reading tour books.

"Well, looks like our adventure ends here, in the Cour Carrée of the Louvre. Do you know anything about it?" I asked Brigitte. "Molière told us a few things, but he didn't have time to tell us everything."

"I'll do my best," said Brigitte, pulling a small guidebook of Paris from her pocket. "If we hadn't met Monsieur Molière we would have had to make do with this. Let's see . . ." she leafed through the pages. "Here it says that the Louvre was originally built as a fortress and had an imposing bastion at the center. It was renovated in Italian **Renaissance** style by Catherine de' Medici, just like Molière said. In the Cour Carrée," Brigitte continued reading, "there is an alternation of vertical and horizontal pavilions with subdued forms and elegant decorations. It was designed by the architect Le Vau, who also renovated Versailles."

"Stop there," I said. "Molière's explanations wouldn't have gone any further. But before heading to the subway station and going home, let's treat ourselves to some giant ice cream cones."

15

The Age of Louis XIV

On September 5, 1638, midwife Madame Péronne delivered a 9-pound (4-kg) infant at the Castle of Saint-Germain-en-Laye, about 12 miles (19 km) west of Paris: it was the future king of France, Louis XIV. She presented him triumphantly to the Louis XIII and the court that, as etiquette demanded, had been present in the royal chamber as the queen gave birth. The bells of Notre Dame rang out wildly. The cannon fired 121 shots. Fifty couriers galloped away on their horses to take the news of the birth of the dauphin (prince) to every corner of France. They had been waiting twenty years for an heir to the throne. The prince was officially baptized several years later, when Louis XIII was gravely ill and close to death. "What's your name, now?" his father asked him after the ceremony. "Louis XIV," answered the child with confidence. "Not yet, my son," the king, reproved him with a hollow voice. Louis was only four-and-a-half years old, but he was already enamored of power.

He could not, however, exercise power until he was twenty-two because his father placed the boy under the guardianship of his mother, Anne of Austria, and **Cardinal Mazarin**, the omnipotent and despised prime minister. In 1649 the high aristocrats revolted against the excessive power of the cardinal. The revolt was called the **Fronde**. Mazarin had to flee to Cologne, while the regent queen and the young king withdrew to the castle of Saint-Germain. The rebel nobles were defeated and the aristocratic front quickly dissolved, but young Louis never forgot the fear he felt during the revolt. Mazarin returned to power in France and made decisions regarding both European policies and the private life of the king, such as arranging the marriage, which was more a political union, to Maria Teresa of Spain.

Mazarin died in March 1661. "Thank God he's finally dropped dead!" These words, attributed to the princess Maria Mancini, the cardinal's niece, reflect the feelings of almost the entire aristocracy. Louis XIV refused to replace him and declared to the Council of the Crown that he would be his own prime minister. He was twenty-two and had been insulted by the Fronde, inherited a powerful France, and been taught by an excellent teacher. He knew he could do it. Louis ordered his secretaries of state not to sign any documents until they had received orders from him personally; every day he was updated on the affairs of state and of normal administration. Alone at the helm, Louis XIV surrounded himself with a handful of able collaborators, such as Colbert, his finance minister. Those who were corrupt and power-hungry were deprived of their authority and eliminated.

Louis XIV did not love Paris, stronghold of the Fronde, but he loved everything that was grand and splendid. He created Versailles, an enchanted place, marvel of regal France, and a concrete symbol of the ostentatious, absolute power of Louis XIV, who had been nicknamed the Sun King. And the Sun King shone with his own light. Louis was powerful, cultured, elegant, and even handsome. Ladies swooned over him. Louis's days in Versailles were characterized by parties, balls, games, tournaments, and the theater. In the gardens he took turns courting the loveliest young women in the kingdom and playing with his beloved dogs: Pistolet, Sylvie, Mignonne, Princesse, and Dorinde.

The Sun King died at Versailles on September 1, 1715, four days before his seventy-seventh birthday. He had reigned for seventy-one years. Louise XIV was buried in the basilica of Saint-Denis in Paris but, when the French revolution broke out in 1789, his remains were thrown into a common grave together with those of his parents, Louis XIII and Anne of Austria.

Below: The Sun King walked in the gardens at Versailles when he was there. This painting by Russian artist Aleksandr Benois, who lived in Paris in the 1930s, depicts Louis and his entourage.

Chronology

ca. 300 BCE – The Parisii, a Gallic tribe, build a log fort on the ford at the isle in the Seine. It was called *Lutetia* ("mid-water dwelling") in Roman times.

52 BCE – Labienus, Julius Caesar's general, conquers Lutetia and rebuilds the fort with stone. The Roman governor sets up his headquarters on the island (Cité) and the city starts to develop on the left bank. A temple to Mars (in present-day Montmartre) is the only thing on the right bank at the time.

250 CE – The first bishop, Dionysius (Saint Denis), is martyred. Christianity spreads.

275 – After three centuries of Roman peace (*Pax Romana*) Lutetia is invaded by another Gallic tribe. The citadel is reinforced and named Paris.

508 – The Salian Franks, led by Clovis, take over Paris and make it their capital.

511–558 – The first church of Notre Dame is built.

752 – Pippin the Short, founder of the Carolingian dynasty, is crowned in Paris at the abbey of Saint-Denis.

885 – The Normans lay siege to Paris and conquer the region then known as Normandy.

987 – Hugh Capet is crowned king, beginning the Capetian dynasty, which remains on the throne of France until the French Revolution.

1163 – Notre Dame is replaced by a new, **Gothic** style church.

1215 – The University of Paris (the Sorbonne), famous for its studies in theology, is founded.

1348 – Half the population of Paris dies in an epidemic of the **plague**.

1420 – The English occupy Paris during the Hundred Years War.

1431 – Joan of Arc is executed.

1528 – The new Louvre is built. Francis I establishes his court in Paris.

1572 – Saint Bartholomew's Day Massacre: a Roman Catholic mob massacres the **Huguenots**; it was supposedly instigated by Catherine de' Medici.

1594 – Paris submits to the Huguenot king Henry IV after his conversion to Roman Catholicism.

1606 – Place des Vosges is built.

1610 – Henry IV is assassinated.

1624–1642 – Cardinal Richelieu, the prime minister, governs France.

1648 – The Fronde against Mazarin and Anne of Austria.

1666 – Louis XIV moves to Versailles.

1715 – Death of Louis XIV.

1751–1772 – Publication of the *Encyclopédie*, a monumental work of the French enlightenment.

1789 – The citizens of Paris take the Bastille by force (July 14 is later proclaimed a national holiday) and the French Revolution begins.

1793 – Louis XVI is beheaded.

1804 – Napoleon Bonaparte is crowned emperor in Notre Dame.

1815 – The Congress of Vienna cancels all of Napoleon's conquests. The old dynasty is restored in France with Louis XVIII.

1830 – Insurrection against Charles X, brother and successor to Louis XVIII; Louis Philippe takes the throne.

1836 – Inauguration of the Arc de Triomphe on the Champs-Elysées.

1851 – Coup d'état by Louis Napoleon Bonaparte (Napoleon III). Beginning of the Second Empire.

1853 – Paris is rebuilt according to plans by Baron Haussmann.

1860 – Paris is divided into 20 districts (*arrondissements*).

1870 – Napoleon III is defeated by the Prussians at Sedan. End of the Second Empire.

1875 – Inauguration of the Opéra in Paris.

1889 – World Fair in Paris for the first centennial celebration of the French Revolution. The Eiffel Tower is built.

1895 – The Lumière brothers invent motion pictures.

1900 – Construction of the Paris subway (metro) is begun.

1914 – World War I begins.

1921 – The population of Paris is 3 million.

1940 – The Germans occupy Paris at the beginning of World War II.

1944 – Liberation of Paris.

1960 – First project for the new district of the Défense.

1962 – Thanks to the Malraux law, Paris renovates its old districts, such as the Marais.

1968 – The Student Revolution: protests by students and workers break out in May.

1969 – The great international competition for the creation of the Beaubourg cultural center is declared. The winning projects are by the Renzo Piano of Italy and the Richard Rogers of England.

1970 – Paris and its urban areas have 10 million inhabitants.

1979 – The remodeling of Les Halles quarter begins.

1997 – The Grand Louvre renovation project, including with the glass Inverted Pyramid by the Chinese architect Pei, is complete.

Glossary

anagram, a word or phrase created by transposing the letters of another word or phrase.

apse, semicircular or polygonal part of the church at the end of the nave, often containing the choir and altar.

Bonaparte, Napoleon (1769–1821), Napoleon I. After supporting the Revolution of 1789 he had himself elected consul for life in 1799 and then crowned emperor in 1804. All the European powers united against him to stop the French expansion throughout Europe and finally defeated him in 1815 at Waterloo. He was exiled to the island of Saint Helena, where he died in 1821.

Colbert, Jean-Baptiste (1619–1683), minister of finance under Louis XIV. He organized the centralized administration of the state and favored the economic reconstruction of French industry.

de' Medici, Catherine (1519–1588), Florentine who became queen of France when she married Henry II and served as was regent (1560) for her son Charles IX. She supposedly ordered the St. Bartholomew's Day Massacre (1572).

de' Medici, Marie (1575–1642), Italian aristocrat who became the second wife of King Henry IV and was regent for her son Louis XIII.

écu, an old French coin.

French Revolution (1789–1799), a revolt by the middle classes in France in the name of liberty, fraternity, and equality. The monarchy and feudal privileges were abolished, the rights of man and the citizen were proclaimed, and the first republic was established.

Fronde, name derived from the French term for "slingshot," used by children in games. The Frondes were a series of civil disturbances that began as a reaction to the policies of Richelieu.

Gothic, art style that flourished in Europe from the 12th- to the 15th-century. The architecture has pointed arches and flying buttresses, ribbed cross vaulting, stained glass, pinnacles, and spires.

Haussmann, Baron Eugène (1809–1891), prefect of the Seine district commissioned by Napoleon III to create an urban plan for Paris. The plan called for the creation of spacious boulevards and large squares.

Henry II (1519–1559), king of France. He was the son of Francis I and husband of Catherine de' Medici. Henry was accidentally killed in a tournament.

Henry IV (1553–1610), a leader of the French Huguenots. He had to convert to Catholicism before ascending the throne. As king, he granted freedom of worship to the Protestants with the Edict of Nantes. His grandson, Louis XIV, revoked the edict.

hôtel, large house or mansion.

Huguenots, French Protestants who suffered persecution for their beliefs in the 16th and 17th centuries.

Île-de-France, historical region of northern France, crossed by the Seine and its tributaries. Paris is in the central part of the Île-de-France.

Jesuits, religious order (Society of Jesus), founded by Saint Ignatius of Loyola (1491–1556) to spread Christianity with missionary works and education. In the 17th century the Jesuit schools were the most modern in Europe.

left bank, area on the left bank of the Seine in Paris, popular with students and artists.

Louis IX, (1215–1270), participated in the 7th Crusade, where he was defeated and taken prisoner, and in the 8th, during which he died of the plague in Tunisia. He was canonized in 1297.

Louis XIII (1601–1643), son of King Henry IV and Marie de' Médici. His prime minister was the Cardinal Richelieu, who restored absolute authority to the monarchy.

Lully Giovanni Battista di Lulli (1632–1687), French composer and musician of Italian birth. He had a splendid career at the court of Louis XIV.

Mazarin, Cardinal Jules (1602–1661), prime minister and regent until Louis XIV came of age. He laid the foundations for French supremacy in Europe and reinforced the absolute monarchy despite the opposition of the parliament and the aristocracy (the Fronde).

Napoleon III, Louis-Napoléon Bonaparte (1808–1873), nephew of Napoleon I, he was the first president of the Second Republic, then emperor in 1812.

plague, infectious and highly contagious disease accidentally transmitted to man by fleas that were infected by diseased rats. Symptoms include fever and swelling of the lymph glands (bubonic plague) or pneumonia symptoms (lung plague). Also known as the Black Death.

reliquary, a container for religious relics, such as the bones of saints.

Renaissance, historical period between the late 14th century and the middle of the 16th century, characterized by the affirmation of a new ideal of life and the rebirth of studies and art. It started in Italy.

stocks, or pillory, a wooden frame in which people were imprisoned and put on public view.

Triton, Greek god who was part man and part fish; also the three-pronged staff he holds.

vault, roofing structure with a curved surface. The simplest is the barrel vault, in the shape of a half cylinder. The cross vault uses two crossing barrel vaults.

Index

Page numbers in **boldface** are illustrations, tables, and charts.

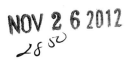